ABUNDANT TRUTH INTERNATIONAL MINISTRIES

Christian Living Series

Keys to Ministry

Discovering the Foundation for Service and Ministry in the Church

Mister Roderick L. Evans

Keys to Ministry

Discovering the Foundation for Service and Ministry in the Church

All Rights reserved ©2024 by Roderick L. Evans

No part of this book may be reproduced or transmitted in any form or by any means, graphic, electronic, or mechanical, including photocopying, recording, taping, or by any information storage or retrieval system, without the permission in writing from the publisher.

Front & Back Cover Designs by Abundant Truth Publishing Free-use Cover Image

Abundant Truth Publishing
an imprint of Abundant Truth International Ministries
For information address:
Abundant Truth International
P.O. Box 126
Camden, NC 27921

ISBN: 978-1-60141-632-2

Printed in the United States of America.

Unless otherwise identified all scripture quotations are from the Authorized *King James Version* of the Bible. Scripture quotations marked with NIV are taken from the *New International Version* of the Bible. Scripture quotations marked with ASV are taken from the *American Standard Version* of the Bible. Scripture quotations marked with GW are taken from the *God's Word Bible*.

Contents

Introduction

Chapter 1 - Origin of Man   1
The Desire of God   5
The Destiny of Man   6

Chapter 2 - Obstinance of Man   11
The Standard of Adam   15
The Redemption of Mankind   16

Chapter 3 - Obedience of Man   21
The Cause of Christ   25
The Conformity of Man   27

Chapter 4 - Obstacles of Man   33
Submission   37
Spiritual Endeavors   39
Closing Thoughts   43

Contents (cont.)

Bibliography 49
Appendix 53

Introduction

Christians are called to the new life in Christ. In addition, service is to accompany that new life. The Christian Living Series is designed to give Christians a biblical perspective to Christian life and service.

In this publication:

God's mandate for ministry in the kingdom begins with character. God gives us the authority and ability to minister to help others mature and grow in Him.

Ministry brings mankind back to God's original plan for them. His original plan was to have sons and daughters. However, man fell through disobedience and God had to provide another way for man to be conformed to His likeness and image.

In this publication, we will examine man's origin, man's obstinance, man's obedience, and man's obstacles to engaging in fruitful ministry and service. It is with this understanding that we can form the proper foundation to comprehend God's mandate for ministry.

KEYS TO MINISTRY

-Chapter 1-
Origin of Man

KEYS TO MINISTRY

And God said, Let us make man in our image, after our likeness: and let them have dominion over the fish of the sea, and over the fowl of the air, and over the cattle, and over all the earth, and over every creeping thing that creepeth upon the earth. (Genesis 1:26)

KEYS TO MINISTRY

In the beginning, God plainly stated His purpose for creating man.

The Desire of God

He wanted man to have His likeness and image and have dominion and authority over all that He created.

And God said, Let us make man in our image, after our likeness: and let them have dominion over the fish of the sea, and over the fowl of the air, and over the cattle, and over all the earth, and over every creeping thing that creepeth upon the earth. (Genesis 1:26)

God's intent was for man to be like Him. When Adam was created, he was made in express image of God.

The Destiny of Man

God's intent has not changed. Therefore, when Adam failed, God sent the last Adam who would bring man back into the presence of God and fulfill the plan of creation: have man in God's likeness and image. We know that Christ came in the image of God. He states,

> *Jesus saith unto him, have I been so long time with you, and yet hast thou not known me, Philip? He that hath*

seen me hath seen the Father; and how sayest thou then, Shew us the Father? (John 14:9)

Jesus came to redeem man. His life is our example. He told Philip that if they had seen Him, they had seen the Father.

In the Garden, God created man like Himself and gave him a charge. He was to have dominion over all that was in the earth. Today, we find that creation rebels against man.

In addition, we find that though man was destined to walk in dominion, he walks in bondage to many influences. Therefore,

KEYS TO MINISTRY

God places the ability to minister in man to facilitate deliverance.

Notes:

KEYS TO MINISTRY

-Chapter 2-
Obstinance of Man

KEYS TO MINISTRY

For thou art an holy people unto the Lord thy God: the Lord thy God hath chosen thee to be a special people unto himself, above all people that are upon the face of the earth. (Deuteronomy 7:6)

KEYS TO MINISTRY

God created man in all righteousness. However, we find that man was corrupted through disobedience. This resulted in generations of people who walked in disobedience and lived lives that were void of purpose and communion with God.

The Standard of Adam

That same Adam, who was to be the standard for all creation after him, disobeyed God.

And unto Adam he said, Because thou hast hearkened unto the voice of thy wife, and hast eaten of the tree, of which I commanded thee, saying, Thou shalt not eat of it: cursed is the ground for thy sake; in sorrow shalt thou eat of it all the days of thy life. (Genesis 3:17)

Man's fall resulted in a curse, whereby all that followed were affected. Men and women born in the earth became vulnerable to the trappings of sin and evil. Though man fell, God's plan and purpose for creating him never changed.

The Redemption of Mankind

Consequently, man's corruption needed a remedy. Therefore, God chose Israel to be His light in the earth. Through their obedience to God, all the nations of the earth would turn to God and be as He originally ordained.

> *For thou art an holy people unto the Lord thy God: the Lord thy God hath chosen thee to be a special people unto himself, above all people that are upon the face of the earth. (Deuteronomy 7:6)*

Though they were to be a light to the Gentiles as God's chosen people, they continually rebelled against God. Therefore, God had to intervene again for the salvation of man. Even though they failed, God's original plan for man to be made in His image remained.

Notes:

KEYS TO MINISTRY

-Chapter 3-
Obedience of Man

KEYS TO MINISTRY

For whom he did foreknow, he also did predestinate to be conformed to the image of his Son, that he might be the firstborn among many brethren. (Romans 8:30)

KEYS TO MINISTRY

God established the New Covenant upon the person and work of Christ. Because of man's corruption, God had to give men the ability to be conformed to His image and likeness.

The Cause of Christ

Christ came in the likeness of sinful flesh in order to deliver men from the bondage of sin.

For what the law could not do, in that it was weak through the flesh, God sending his own Son in the likeness of sinful flesh, and for sin, condemned sin in the flesh: That the righteousness of the law might be fulfilled in us, who walk not after the flesh, but after the Spirit. (Romans 8:3-4)

The above scripture states that the result of His coming was that the righteousness of the law (God's standard for man) could be fulfilled or completed in men. The indwelling presence of the Spirit gives men the ability to fulfill the predestined will of God.

For whom he did foreknow, he also did predestinate to be conformed to the image of his Son, that he might be the firstborn among many brethren. (Romans 8:30)

The Conformity of Man

The will of God is for men and women to be conformed to the image of Jesus Christ. He places individuals in ministry to perform this task.

When Paul listed the ministry offices as recorded in Ephesians 4, he states that their purpose is to cause the Church to come into the fullness of Christ's personality, not just His power.

His intention was the perfecting and the full equipping of the saints (His consecrated people), [that they should do] the work of the ministering toward building up Christ's body (the Church), [that it might develop] until we attain oneness in the faith and in the comprehension of the full and accurate knowledge of the Son of God; that [we might arrive] at really mature manhood – standard height of Christ's own perfection – the measure of the stature of the fullness of the Christ, and the completeness found in Him. (Ephesians 4:12-13 Amplified)

God intended for ministers to develop mature believers who reflect the nature of Christ. Ministry and gifts are given to help men conform to the image of God. Our gifts are to be used for this intent. We must remember that all ministry points to Christ, not ourselves.

KEYS TO MINISTRY

Notes:

_____

_____

_____

_____

_____

_____

_____

_____

KEYS TO MINISTRY

-Chapter 4-

Obstacles of Man

KEYS TO MINISTRY

KEYS TO MINISTRY

The sheep that are My own hear and to My voice, and I know them and they follow Me.

(John 10:27 Amplified)

KEYS TO MINISTRY

After we have received Christ in our lives, one of the main obstacles that faces Vus is submission to ministry. If we cannot meet this challenge, we will fail before we get started.

Submission

Ministry does not begin with preaching a sermon, laying hands, prophesying, or praying. Ministry begins in us as we submit to the ministry of the Spirit.

Before we can minister, we first must receive ministry. The ministry of the Spirit is designed to make us like Christ.

Without allowing the Spirit to minister to us, we will not be effective in ministry.

The question remains, "How do Spirit?" We submit to His ministry in two ways. First, we submit to Him by following the leading of His indwelling presence.

The Spirit of God comes to lead and guide us into all truth. He not only leads us into truth concerning doctrine, but also into the truth about our personal weaknesses and hindrances.

Without submitting to His voice in our personal relationship with Him, it will be almost impossible to follow His voice in a ministry setting.

To follow His inner leading is not as difficult as some have made it. Jesus said that His sheep hears (knows) His voice.

The sheep that are My own hear and to My voice, and I know them and they follow Me. (John 10:27 Amplified)

Spiritual Endeavors

Consistent prayer and study of the Word help the believer to know the voice of the Holy Spirit. When we are able to recognize His voice, we then have to follow His directives.

The second way we submit to the Holy Spirit is by following His instructions through others.

The Holy Spirit not only speaks tous personally, but He speaks to us through others. The Spirit of God releases gifts and ministries upon members of the Body of Christ for its edification.

> *But to each one is given the manifestation of the (Holy) Spirit – that is, the evidence, the spiritual illumination of the Spirit – for good*

and profit. (I Corinthians 12:7 Amplified)

We have to receive the gifts that God has placed in others for our benefit. If we learn to receive ministry, others will receive ministry from us. This is the beginning of ministry.

The challenge then remains for us to consistently receive ministry, which prepares us to minister. We receive ministry to develop His nature. When we are like Him, we will do His works.

God, who at sundry times and in divers manners spake in time past unto the fathers by the prophets, Hath in these last days spoken unto us by his Son, whom he hath appointed heir of all things, by whom also he made the worlds. (Hebrews 1:1-2)

The writer of Hebrews says that in these last days God speaks to us through His Son. When we are like the Son, God can speak through us. He can then use us.

The character of Christ produces kingdom ministry. Without His nature, the proper foundation for ministry in the kingdom is not laid.

Closing Thoughts for the Kingdom Mandate for Ministry

- From the beginning, God's plan was to have sons and daughters.

- Therefore, the Spirit of God comes to help us reflect His very nature and character.

- If we possess His nature, we will do His works.

- When we become like Christ, we will be able to do the greater works that He spoke of.

KEYS TO MINISTRY

- ➢ We must remember that before we can minister effectively, we must submit to ministry.

- ➢ The ministry of the Spirit will come from His inner voice and through others.

- ➢ The Lord does all of this so that men can be conformed to Christ's image.

- ➢ There is no other foundation for ministry except to be like God.

- ➢ For a full examination of God's purpose for ministry, please see my book, "He Gave Gifts Unto Men: God's Mandate for Ministry in the Kingdom."

Notes:

KEYS TO MINISTRY

Bibliography

Smith, William. *Smith's Bible Dictionary.* Holman Bible Publishers. Nashville, Tennessee. c1994

The Bible Library. *The Bible Library CD Rom Disc.* Ellis Enterprises Incorporated, (c)1988 – 2000. 4205 McAuley Blvd., Suite 385, Oklahoma City, OK 73120. All Rights Reserved.

Lockman Foundation. *Comparative Study Bible.* Zondervan Publishing House. Grand Rapids, MI, c1984

Notes:

KEYS TO MINISTRY

Appendix

The ministry of the teacher and gifts of the Spirit are a source of controversy and excitement. This appendix lists some popular passages of scriptures concerning ministries and gifts. These are given to inspire others to research this topic.

KEYS TO MINISTRY

The Outpouring of the Spirit (Acts 2:17-18)

17. And it shall come to pass in the last days, saith God, I will pour out of my Spirit upon all flesh: and your sons and your daughters shall prophesy, and your young men shall see visions, and your old men shall dream dreams: 18. And on my servants and on my handmaidens I will pour out in those days of my Spirit; and they shall prophesy:

KEYS TO MINISTRY

The Nine Gifts of the Spirit (I Corinthians 12:4-11)

4. Now there are diversities of gifts, but the same Spirit.

5. And there are differences of administrations, but the same Lord.

6. And there are diversities of operations, but it is the same God which worketh all in all.

7. But the manifestation of the Spirit is given to every man to profit withal.

8. For to one is given by the Spirit the word of wisdom; to another the word of

knowledge by the same Spirit;

9. To another faith by the same Spirit; to another the gifts of healing by the same Spirit;

10. To another the working of miracles; to another prophecy; to another discerning of spirits; to another divers kinds of tongues; to another the interpretation of tongues:

11. But all these worketh that one and the selfsame Spirit, dividing to every man severally as he will.

The Setting of Gifts in the Church (I Corinthians 12:27-28)

27. Now ye are the body of Christ, and members in particular.

28. And God hath set some in the church, first apostles, secondarily prophets, thirdly teachers, after that miracles, then gifts of healings, helps, governments, diversities of tongues.

KEYS TO MINISTRY

The Gift of Togues versus Prophecy (I Corinthians 14:1-9)

1. Follow after charity, and desire spiritual gifts, but rather that ye may prophesy.

2. For he that speaketh in an unknown tongue

speaketh not unto men, but unto God: for no man understandeth him; howbeit in the spirit he speaketh mysteries.

3. But he that prophesieth speaketh unto men to edification, and exhortation, and comfort.

4. He that speaketh in an unknown

tongue edifieth himself; but he that prophesieth edifieth the church.

5. I would that ye all spake with tongues; but rather that ye prophesied: for greater is he that prophesieth than he that speaketh with tongues, except he interpret, that the church may receive edifying.

6. Now, brethren, if I come unto you speaking with tongues, what shall I profit you, except I shall speak to you either by revelation, or by knowledge, or by prophesying, or by doctrine?

7. And even things without life giving sound, whether pipe or harp, except

they give a distinction in the sounds, how shall it be known what is piped or harped?

8. For if the trumpet give an uncertain sound, who shall prepare himself to the battle?

9. So likewise ye, except ye utter by the tongue words easy to be understood, how shall it be known what is spoken? for ye shall speak into the air.

KEYS TO MINISTRY

The Ministry Gifts and Purpose (Ephesians 4:11-15)

11. And he gave some, apostles; and some, prophets; and some, evangelists; and some, pastors and teachers;

12. For the perfecting of the saints, for the work of the ministry, for the edifying of the body of Christ:

13. Till we all come in the unity of the faith, and of the knowledge of the Son of God, unto a perfect man, unto the measure of the stature of the fullness of Christ:

14. That we henceforth be no more children, tossed to and fro, and carried about with every wind of doctrine, by the sleight of men, and cunning craftiness, whereby they lie in wait to deceive;

15. But speaking the truth in love, may grow up into him in all things, which is the head, even Christ:

15. But speaking the truth in love, may grow up into him in all things, which is the head, even Christ:

Notes:

KEYS TO MINISTRY

Notes:

KEYS TO MINISTRY

www.ingramcontent.com/pod-product-compliance
Lightning Source LLC
Chambersburg PA
CBHW050344010526
44119CB00049B/685